The Inner View

The Inner View

SPIRIT FINDER

BALBOA.
PRESS

A DIVISION OF HAY HOUSE

Balboa Press books may be ordered through booksellers or by contacting:

Balboa Press
A Division of Hay House
1663 Liberty Drive
Bloomington, IN 47403
www.balboapress.com
1-(877) 407-4847

ISBN: 978-1-4525-0856-6 (sc)
ISBN: 978-1-4525-0857-3 (e)

Balboa Press rev. date: 1/31/2013

Contents

Preface

I was interested in spirit from a very early age. Church to me was a place of refuge where you could be silent and go within to a place of quiet contemplation. As I grew older I became more critical of my church as I saw it's behavior and attitudes didn't live up to the teachings of Jesus Christ. After a short period of no belief at all in my early twenties, my interest shifted to meditation and what it could offer.

This, I felt, was a way to live life more truthfully and from there grew an interest in all religions, especially those that encouraged inquiry and kindness to all mankind.

As one great master said: "Prayer is when you are talking to God. Meditation is when God is talking to you".

This was the beginning of a quest or pilgrimage that took me to many outstanding masters over many years. I needed to learn my lessons from many teachers. Many people live life very happily with one faith and teaching for their entire life and are very content with this. And it is no doubt right for them.

I found myself with very little knowledge just knowing I had to go and spend time with the masters of the east. Buddhism and Hinduism were my main points of call but the quest took me to other avenues of self-inquiry. Facing my fears on zip lines and trekking in the Himalayas and the Andes also revealed some inner treasures.

I wanted to know and understand the answer to life's most fundamental questions—like who am I and what was the meaning of life, and yes I learned much from teachers and wonderful energetic environments but it was to be through meditation that my biggest breakthroughs emerged.

Sometimes it was experiencing the bliss that surpasses all understanding and other times it showed me where my behavior was not appropriate and in time where it came from.

Meditation was like a trickle of water cutting its way through the bank slowly over many years until it became a river. By degrees you discover your own truth and begin to listen and act on those inner promptings and yearnings.

It would be wrong of me to suggest I was bonded to my inner lover all the time. Definitely not. I have had many, many years of being out of balance and out of step with the generous flow of life.

But even in the roughest times I knew what I needed to do and often that meant just being with whatever was being made wrong in me or someone else until forgiveness arose and I could move on.

Then, and only then, could I get back to my meditation.

I hope these poems or jottings, that revealed themselves when I was deeply relaxed when traveling or meditating or after some rugged self-inquiry, may encourage anyone who reads them to take their own inner journey . . . to learn to listen to their own inner teacher, their own voice of wisdom.

Go straight to the well of truth in your own being, have your own experience . . . Trust that. I wish you well.

—Dianna Kett

The Blessed Boy

He was small for his age, no shoes on his feet.
So skilled was his English that he captured our minds as we walked.
We learned that this curly-haired
child had left his home of Calcutta six years ago.
Since he was 10 he had lived by his wits on the street.

His bright eyes and personable chatter
beguiled us so much that we paid too dearly for his garlands of flowers.
The next day I met, him alone,
this was a different boy from yesterday.
I learned of dashed dreams and hopes,
that drove him to the streets each day.

Would I make love with him, he asked
while I felt such quiet dread.
My voice belied my fear as I replied:
we were not the right age.

He asked of my children whom I'd left in their home.
As I finished my reply we were walking neither looking at the other.
I felt a jolt of pain before he spoke,
I'm tired and I'm hungry,
I want someone to look after me, he cried.

My body was wanting to flee from this boy who had prised open my
heart with his tender young claws.
My feet were moving away, I wanted to run.
But it was too late, the damage was done,
I'd seen to my cost
that he had reflected back my own inner pain and loss.

Was it conscience or a need of clarity that had me searching for him
on my last night in Delhi,
I will probably never know.
I rounded the corner to the shops that were his stamping ground,
it wasn't long before we met.

This time he was wearing a beggar's dress,
but his bright eyes belied the lie.
He grabbed some flowers from the seller,
and gave me some as he walked alongside,
talking of a German 1over he had known.

I asked him of his schooling and found he had had none,
I can write my name, was his only reply.
I want money for a blanket was all he said,
I gave him some rupees and said goodbye.
My pain was spent,
who was I to ask at what cost?

But he was a blessed boy,
he'd shown me more about human strength than I'd ever seen before.
That the diamond can shine even though it is surrounded in mire,
my blessed young prostitute.

The Seeker

India, the place her soul calls home,
where friendly faces openly, directly
communicate with her—the hidden one.
The foreigner !

The foreigner who comes to seek she knows not what,
who has the trappings of a modern lifestyle,
But she has not what?

Her mind is puzzled by her love of what she is not.
The simple smile of no yesterdays,
and no tomorrows greets her everywhere.
And yet she still lies trapped in what she is not.

She muses over how she can cross the bridge
of no tomorrows and no yesterdays.
Her mind dances briefly in some moments,
like it has been released from its cage.

Sometimes the dance comes un-expectantly, in the street,
but she stops for fear of being labeled crazy.
She watches how much joy is felt when her inner bliss takes flight.

Sometimes it comes when she plays with a child,
the laughter and fun of a game for a moment make her mind a servant.

In these moments of grace she feels at one with the bliss of the simple life,
and her seeking stops.

3

The Watcher

The simple Indian waiter watches me, and I watch him.
Two very different cultures,
the watcher watching the watcher.
The food comes, the waves crash on the beach below,
I know this is paradise.
But my mind struggles with this contentment,
he lives here this waiter and has served many westerners like me.
But I see his curiousity. And he sees mine.

The Underground

This London Underground,
People rushing down steps with their eyes downcast,
I feel the flurry of energy as they pass.
But as I watch I am aware that I am invisible,
I could be from another planet.
These faces so downcast and intent on their journey,
that the moment of traveling is lost.
A place where time is so precious,
and yet it is wasted,
I too can move in this unconscious state,
but am aware of what is lost.

Who is Pleased?

Sitting listening to the waves crash onto the shore and the
conversation next door.
The Muslim shop owner was upset,
she had not been to see his wares.
She had told him she would see them when she came back in March,
but he was peeved.
Her mind did not care,
the pen was running,
She had just learned an important lesson,
that she didn't have to please everybody all the time.
Ah, the peace and bliss of this.

The Englishwoman

Tall and thin,
with that soft peaches and cream complexion.
A straightness in her communication,
and a loving that peeps from her eyes and the corners of her mouth.
So far from the land of her ancestors,
and yet so at home.
The music, the color, the scent,
the madness of an Indian continent.
It has her heart,
and she asks no questions.

Massage with a Message

Evening:
She'd come for her second massage,
not really wanting it but determined to keep her word.
The young masseur asked the normal questions.
When he discovered she was divorced he said: divorce is very bad.
"Sometimes," she replied, "but not always."
He asked her age. She replied 47 and asked him his.
He was 24.
She wondered at such strong views from someone so young,
so sure of his opinion.
She told him he couldn't know anything until he had experienced it,
she felt his bewilderment and realised his views came from old rules
and culture.
Not that his views are wrong, she thought.
But they are not HIS views.

The Sound of Silence

Outside the ashram gates the noise of India competed loudly,
shouts of rupees, rupees, accompanied the begging hand, while dust and
traffic just added to the din.

The devotees had stepped out of the peaceful confines of grace,
into the busy street to sip some chai at a food stall.
So many restrictions and so much quiet, had them bursting with talk
about their experience.

In the tight band they sat, eating in a flurry of chat. No one noticed the
holy man, come forward with his begging bowl outstretched.

But she looked up at the man with the dreadlocks,
numbed by the quite of this renunciate in this crowd,
and found his silence deafening.
For a moment their eyes met, and then he backed away,
from this circus of spirituality.

The Fishermen still Live as You

Going to church, old memories of at-one-ment.
Hearing the words,
and feeling their real meaning.
Not what was said,
but a knowing of what these words really meant.
Being God's witness, not separate.
God's will,
shining so brightly,
through these forms that are not who we are.
Beaming auras, that silently spread the word.
That the word is God.
Nothing to do, but to reflect back to what is Omnipresent.
And seeing, real seeing,
of who really choses,
and who really acts.
To be a puppet on the string of truth.
No free will,
but Divine will manifest in a human form.
No false humility,
but a burning to ashes of all delusions and beliefs.
How many times have we looked for love in all the wrong places.
But inside of us, lies out greatest friend,
our best lover, our creative genius,
our compassionate Buddha,
our suffering Christ.
Closer than our own breath,
breathing as you.

—Paris' first communion, May 1999.

Deeper and Deeper it Pulls . . .

This love, this pull,
sometimes it catches fire.
This beloved has me so entranced,
and aching for love,
that all outside distractions fade into nothingness.
Deeper and deeper it pulls, and I am entwined.
Impossible to disentangle, from this that is me at my core.
My total attention, and every breath is for breathing this.
This fire of purity and bliss.

Dancing in the Light

Dancing in a whirl, round and round.
her eyes were closed.
Watching that elusive light just out of her reach.
The pulsating glow had her head turning,
in hot pursuit.
So many times she had danced,
and so many times,
this light flashed into her third-eye vision.
But today she wanted more,
tired of the chase,
she asked the light to come to her,
to stop flashing out of her reach.
She moved to the music,
and suddenly a big light appeared,
she was swaying, ecstatic,
and the light stayed.
Closer and closer it came,
until it merged.
She and the light became one.

Awakenings

Awakenings,
to what is true.
Nobody here,
nothing to do.
Such love,
from an invisible source.
That heals, cajoles,
and slaps,
till the sleeping one wakes up.
Lost in the mind,
lost to the self.
And then,
a fingersnap points to what is real.
All is perfect,
just as it is.
And gratitude grows,
from that invisible source.
The one that forgot from whence she came,
is once again conscious of her own divinity

To Understand

To understand is a gift,
that is little understood.
Some part of the puzzle falls into place,
for this member of the human race.
Revelations are of this day and time,
not stuck in some past of old lang syne.

Yet, to be understood, transforms one's soul,
and brings on a smile to lighten the mile.
A beautiful glow radiates out from the chest,
one can hardly breathe.
This heart feels too full,
almost bursting with this contentment.

So Much Fullness

I wonder why sleep doesn't come,
some urge to write something.
A restlessness,
after such a bliss-filled evening.
Thoughts powerless,
just falling straight into the waste paper bin.
This silence, so steady, so much love,
any attempt to think lost.
Blank, but not an empty blankness,
so much fullness.
In love,
but more I am love.
So real, so palpable,
seeing an end to a way of life,
and her attempts to find love in all the wrong places.

The Divine Self

A divine song,
not needing anything else.
Nothing to do,
no place to go, at home always
in bliss and pain.
Not even a name
can describe this presence.
It sits as one heart,
beats as one heart,
loves as one heart.
I am that,
forever,
eternally free.

Moonlight Serenade . . .

Moonlight streams across my bed,
a restless need to express is equalled by resistance,
it had been a blissful evening.
No curtain call needed,
this love beyond words.
Making a mockery of the countless attempts made,
to find love outside herself.
How had she missed this?
Years of searching for it and running from it,
all the time she knew it was there.
The young dreamer who was told she would get better marks,
if she concentrated on her work,
and stopped gazing out of the window.
Still there in those blind heady political days,
when she believed if people won't share,
they must be made to share.
What madness,
this external mind-orientated socialism.
Just a belief,
but even then presence was there,
in this earnest quest for equality.
So different now, so changed.
Nothing needs to be done,
nothing needs to change.
Because presence so full,
so boundless, so loving and never changing,
is always, always present.

Mental Illness

Every time you think a bad thought about yourself or anyone else,
that's mental illness.
I don't mean to notice bad behavior in yourself,
or someone else is wrong.
That's natural,
the eyes see, the ears hear.
But when that critical judgment stays in the mind
and goes round and round for days on end,
peace has disappeared,
being present is not possible,
and joy has been obscured from view.
To be happy is not something to be gained by looking outside,
but by diligently watching your own mind.
Moment by moment,
and tracing that thought to its cause.
Before it moves into the body,
as a feeling of anger, jealousy or withdrawal.

Doing Nothing

My mind asks what have you been doing these past two years?
The critical male part of me is scathing.
It answers . . . nothing.
But a more gentle feminine voice has noticed some changes,
very subtle, but deep changes.

Not being so very busy has revealed something not noticed before.
Like that funny little mouse,
that skipped and almost danced across the bricks.
He was an entertainer mouse and his energy was light and happy.
One morning as I sat meditating I opened my eyes,
and there one foot away sat this little mouse looking at me.
He was meditating too, but with his eyes open.
I remember when I feared these funny, furry little creatures.

This world around us can be invisible to the busy.
The mystery of the domestic animal world,
the gifts they give us so freely.
Their feelings, some would call instinct,
come from some deep place.
Another world,
and they attach themselves to us.
Their giving, rather than getting,
pulls the hardened human heart apart and renders it soft and pliable.
As the years go by master and servant become one.

Some mornings my mind is like a whip.
Do something now to make yourself useful, it says.
A lame attempt at action can't win,
as very soon the softness returns and my mind lets things be.
Sometimes it is like a wave of self-anger drowning me,
and then the wave moves back out to sea.
And all is left is this leaf blowing gently in the breeze.

When I feel this desperate need to do something,
I mostly find, I'm running from some feeling inside,
rather than running to something new.
There's something about going fast that represses feeling,
while slowness allows feelings to come to the surface for expression.

Time is of the essence they say.
Some would describe it as a friend,
and others would describe it as a foe.
It depends.
Time is neutral. Time is not the enemy.
Taking time out to allow experiences and feelings,
can be fulfilling to the soul.
There may be some churning and heat,
but the cake can turn out okay.

So when it comes time to give an account,
of my creativity or my earnings,
I can't answer in a swift business-like way.
Life is happening to me every day,
more deeply than when I was busy.
That is all I have to say.

Manipulations

Awoke at 3am, dogs barking, mind racing.
Trying to work it all out, useless exercise going
down tracks to dead ends, over and over again.
Why this night so much fury?
Longing for the sweet balm of sleep,
but the mind relentless in its urging to find some clarity,
down the alleyways of my own madness.
The dogs have stopped, my body twitches and I
wonder whether it is worth turning out the light.

Whitefield, India.

Winter Solstice

My Indian lover behaving really weird, very angry driving to Mysore.
When we arrived at hotel he dropped straight into bed.
Very tired, he said.
I'm just watching,
he's not the same with me and I feel I'm not the same with him.
The fire seems to have gone out, and I'm full of fear.
Next morning we sat opposite each other and he talked:
Said he'd noticed he was not the same with me,
and that he couldn't feel my love like before.
My heart is breaking.
Watching myself break into pieces.
This love that has dominated my life for more than five years just
falling apart.
Why pretend? When the fire is out it is out.
With the talking I just wanted to run away.
But soon my lover is crushing me on the bed making love full of fire.
I too am responding full of fire, open completely to him I am.
We walk out of this expensive hotel,
porters salute me and I feel like an Indian princess, no less.
The man I love has just told me that his love for me has changed.
on the outside it is a mess but on the inside I am in bliss.
There's a part of me that has it's own light that no one can snuff out.
Right in the middle of my terror, my worst fear,
what felt like the end of my life there remained this bubbling bliss.

Another day has passed with the man who had been the love of my life,
a separateness is there, the uncontrollable fire seems spent.
But every now and then a spark turns in the fire and we are
consumed in each other again.
I say to my Indian lover your energy is more like husband now.
He asks: Is that all right?
I smile and say yes it's okay. It will do.I reminisce about this passion . . . .
this quest that has brought the extremes of pain and pleasure.
Where it came from and where it went.
The love spark is free,
who knows where it will spark it's light next.
It can't be bound by habit or beliefs,
any attempt to fence it in is a waste of energy spent.
So my winter solstice ends.

Love is there Every Moment

It was the final drive to the final goodbye,
trying not to think, she was in pain.
Just be the witness, the inner voice said,
he had stopped to take photos of the lotus on the pond.
She stood by the tree looking nowhere, a stranger in a strange culture.
Colorfully clad girls stopped and stared at her,
they came closer.
Dark-skinned with thick hair twisted in long plaits,
their bright faces beaming.
One came close, very close,
she pinched her, the foreigner, on the cheek.
Face-to-face, the open eyes beamed warmly at the pale face,
together they smiled.
Some recognition,
some love from some hidden source flowed.
The foreigner held back her tears,
the girls all smiled and walked off waving as they went.
Yes, love is there every moment; every second,
if you are awake.
Man and camera reappeared,
and the drive continued.

The Final Goodbye

Sitting in the plane en route to Delhi,
feeling cool after the heat of the night before.
Strong words she had spoken to her Indian lover,
about needing something more than his loving embrace.
That something . . . support and consideration,
was not what he could give.
He had sat there quietly while she fired her pain at him,
not saying one word.
With hands clasped and tears in his eyes he finally spoke,
sorry, he said, my love is all I can give you.
She didn't cry,
she'd felt the pain and the hurt.
Her eyes were dry,
and she knew that once again it was time for goodbye.

Remembering . . .

Like a flash it came late at night.
Remembering the one who said:
"You are the one that I want . . .
and before you I did my meditation
and kept all the rules but my heart was dry.
With you I break all the rules and my heart is open."
A karmic dance this man and I,
and like all dances it had to take its final bow.
Now the curtain of forgetfulness,
will fall on the romance of my dreams.

The Dance of Freedom

Sometimes she goes underground, into her own darkness,
and she finds strong currents of feeling there.
The mind buffets her this way and that,
one moment her friend and the next her deadly enemy.

Yet, she is aware that the earth holds her in its sweet embrace,
so she waits.
Knowing that she is held she can sit, and be the watcher,
she knows only too well that scars occur when she makes the drama real.

Quickly she returns to the resting place of the witness,
above her fertility rites are being performed like compost being laid on
top of cold soil.
She knows that like the seed she too will sprout towards the light
when the time is right,
and her season of darkness will give way to a new way of seeing
the mystery of life,
the light, the shade, the movement and the laughter.

Some new freedom she will have found within herself, and she'll rejoice.
Knowing that at any time the current can turn and start to cut away at
the banks of her beliefs,
beliefs that limit and constrain her.
And once again she'll sit, and watch, and wait.

You are What You Seek

The Sanctuary was ready to celebrate,
it was thanksgiving,
a day to relax, a day to give thanks.

We waited for this western meditation master,
whose war was with the enemies within,
rather than with the enemies without.

I wondered about this man,
who had surrendered to be a monk at the
feet of Swami Muktananda many years before.

Yet he had outgrown this Indianness.
Aware of each moment,
no judgment, focussed.
And we were lit up by him.

Attachment and Blame

The Master knows how to journey those who are good at what they do,
he gives them a trouble-free run for while.
One day he puts someone less efficient or less experienced than they
are in charge.
The bright one either laughs or takes it as a joke,
or leaves angry and hurt.
What is being journeyed here is not the qualifications for the job,
but the need of the perfect one to be perfect,
or at least to be seen as such.
No attachment to the result is the lesson here.
Many don't get the message,
they leave and blame everyone else,
for their anger and their unhappiness.

The Dance of the Inner Self

She sat with her eyes closed,
the dance within so entrancing she dared not open her eyes.
She knew they were waiting for the performance,
they had come through the entrance of the theatre in a trance.
Ready to forget for a while,
and they would exit at the end.
It would happen in this small theatre,
as it happens in life.
The watcher and the players, in a trance.
Who would be awake at the exit into ecstasy.
These dreamers so often distracted by what is unreal.
Eyes too open to the outside,
and . . . too closed to themselves.
The dance of their own inner self.

She Felt My Sadness

Went into new Vietnamese noodle shop for lunch,
and had trouble explaining I wanted vegetarian.
No understand, I'm told,
but soon the faces light up when I say fish is okay.
Deep inner workings this day,
and as I eat my lunch the owner's wife sits down next to me.
You okay, she asks.
I say yes, but in my mind I know it is too difficult to explain.
She asks me about family and children. I tell her.
She says I am young to be grandmother.
I thank her, but explain that our ages are about the same.
She moves away and watches me from the distance,
after I pay she puts her arm in mine and walks me to the street.
Such love and compassion from this woman who is a stranger to me,
she felt my sadness.

Powerless Thoughts

I wonder why sleep doesn't come,
some urge to write something.
A restlessness after such a bliss-filled evening,
thoughts powerless falling straight into the waste paper bin.
This silence, so steady, so much love,
any attempt to think lost.
Just blank,
but not an empty blankness,
so much fullness.
In love,
but more I am love.
So real, so palpable,
just seeing an end to a way of life,
and her attempts to find love in all the wrong places.

Questions, Questions . . .

I noticed, at one time, I gave up on bliss,
the pain was too deep that always followed.
But what if the bliss was following the pain,
just see-sawing.
No terror, no pain,
just mind minding too much.
Trying to understand,
then I drop and I stop,
and the questions seem irrelevant,
or forgotten.
This wisp or thread that had me in dread,
has fled and I'm ready for bed.

Uncover the Costumes

Sitting on couch next to male stranger,
I couldn't feel any difference between him and me.
The same self, no identity,
just comfort and sameness.
All that is.
Such a camouflage,
the appearance of diversity.
But uncover the costumes,
of male and female, black and white,
good and bad,
and I find one heart,
beats all these forms.

Seeing the One

Seeing the one that fires us all is one . . .
That IT doesn't have a different current for me,
and something different for someone else.
One current,
which means everyone on earth is my brother and sister,
however they may appear.
The same current my friend sits in,
my form also sits in.
We are not different,
we are not even here.
We are space and how can
space be different or limited.
Space is space,
no mind needed.
Nothing to do and nowhere to go,
no separation is possible.
Different costumes or facades,
but the one light,
that shines through us all.

Journey's End

A once proud lady . . .
shipwrecked on the rocks,
no sails left to blow in the wind.

Many journeys she had taken,
across wild and stormy seas,
but those days were finished.
Firmly she sat,
with waves sometimes crashing,
sometimes tenderly lapping,
against her rotting hulk.

On deck the sun warmed and caressed her,
bleaching white those once shiny boards,
that had lovingly supported all who had walked on her.

But her bright spirit was not in the dilapidated state of her form,
it loved the dark hull,
twinkling with lights shining through the holes and
crevices.

Her spirit danced and laughed while the ship rested.
No more journeys to take,
this stillness she found,
was bliss itself.

The Seeker Returns Home

I went looking for this nameless witness of all that is,
into the ocean of consciousness, the emptiness.
And I looked, and I looked,
I couldn't find me anywhere.
Some disappointment arose in this all pervading peace,
no me, goodness.
My mind stops at the joke,
so much had I identified with the body.
The personality,
so attached to this story of me.
And in one moment,
all that IS reveals,
I don't exist.
Just consciousness~ bubbling bliss,
this body/mind had me tricked.
I am that nothingness~ that stillness~ that peace,
that all pervading bliss.
No more tricks,
no more identity,
no more image.
I surrender to that nothingness,
let it flow through this body /mind,
as it wills.
So I bow this day to this ocean,
I prostrate myself to this truth of being itself.
I can't think this night,
no mind~ just sleep, just rest.
Awoke and found myself resting in that ocean of stillness.

End of Shadow Boxing

IT feels like a ninety per cent shift,
something that I had been pushing away.
Keeping myself safe from,
my shadow-self was coming home to roost.

Those dark parts of me that I kept hidden,
especially from myself.
Were being viewed in a different light.

What if I invite them all home,
and embrace them and thank them for what they have done?
They can stay and be at home,
I see their role in protecting me.
They are my children, why should I make them unwelcome.

But now I choose to live from that grounded space,
where truth lies.
Trusting the spaciousness, openness, and confidence that
comes from who I really am.
I accept that all these emotions are part of the oneness,
but I now choose to go inside to the heart of my being,
. . . and be me.

Turning the Attention Inside

What to do when the disintegration is from the inside out,
when you finally get it that no one is to blame.
All beliefs and old ways of coping lay on the ground,
like rubbish just waiting to be swept up and burned.

Justifying your position on any point now a useless waste of time,
you just can't lie to yourself anymore.
No one outside of you is responsible for your errors, belief patterns and moods,
no one outside of you can love you the way you can love yourself.
Wanting and wishing and waiting,
all ready for the waste bin.

The lies are piled up and they are on the nose,
time to put a match to them all.
All the life experiences and people I judged,
nothing was wrong, with them,
with life or most important of all, with myself.

Now can I let go,
flowing with the breeze.
Enjoying each moment.
Not having to be anything.

It seems so little, it seems so simple.
A death of a kind, nothing to hold on to.
Nothing external, that is.

Loving myself from the inside out.
Every little pain, every little suffering, every little worry.
Turning the attention inside,
gathering my own love force.
Feeling it's intensity,
and wrapping it around any inner disturbance.
Smothering the pain with love from my own being.

And when the eyes see and the heart feels pain in another,
in the form of anger, rudeness, jealousy,
that same cushion of love stored in my heart,
moves out and embraces and holds their pain.

Back I go to my own inner well.
I fill the bucket and head out again,
with love on board.
Ready to wrap and hold that ugly duckling wherever she appears.
That inner lover carries the soft green moss,
to cool that burning pain.
Transmuting pain into love is magical,
there's no more pain.

A Flame of Truth

Dearest Papaji what a flame of truth you are,
cutting through mountains of illusion.
To the core of all being,
on your deathbed as you took your last breath you said:
"Where is the Buddha now? Take me to him! I am ready."
What a flame,
what a torch you threw out to the whole world.
And I am so quiet,
this stillness, has me this day.
No battle,
just surrender to what is.

Magic Mountain of Grace

To leave the city,
even for just one day.
To breathe in the cool air of the mountain.

To catch a chance,
for a long glance.
And behold a glistening world.

Where every leaf,
shines with its own energy and light.

Where tree branches entertwine like beautiful lace,
where nature nestles in peace.

Oh, for the grace to live like this mountain.
Yes, for now it is time to give thanks.

For the dirt is not dirt,
but living, breathing groundedness,
the breeding ground of all things possible.

The Impossible Dream

She would dearly love to soar like an eagle,
and live her life to the fullest.
But, she knows, if she takes off,
those she loves will be lost to her forever.
The risks are so great and the delights so tempting,
her heart beats faster.
Yet . . . she doesn't have the right,
she knows what she is missing.
Somehow with resignation and sadness,
she must go on . . .

IVF Heartbreak

No one sees the pain of the infertile woman,
who not only has to accept the failure herself but must explain it to
her man,
and still feel a woman . . .
a sexually attractive woman.
Migrant women suffer most,
for her, family and procreation are her entitlement to be.
Her face crumples as the doctor explains there is no hope.
Distress engulfs this woman that came in full of hope,
and who left stripped of much more than her dignity.
Another woman watches with her heart open to the pain.
She moves in to comfort her,
and notices that there is nothing so cold as this waiting room.
No one came with a cup of tea, to cheer the migrant woman,
who left a victim of a heartless system.
One that fires a woman's hope every month,
and dashes that joy with the first sign of blood.
She overheard a woman on the IVF program discussing the doctors
and how to handle them.
"You can't show them you are not coping," she whispered.
"Or you'll find they won't consider you for another try."
So emotion and feeling are kept in tight hold.
Until the day comes when hope runs out,
and she, like the migrant woman,
will run away to find a place to hide and cry.

.

Goodbye My Son

I saw something today . . .
The boy she had loved for 20 years,
she didn't notice him grow.
Once day he was the baby impatient to be fed,
the next in uniform, unsure and shy, but ready for school.
Then came the tease, the imp, the recluse,
the one who kicked his mum when things went wrong.
His growing pains, she felt, his sadness, she felt.
She felt his joy when he first fell in love,
and his grief when his heart first broke.
And now today, with another girl in his heart, he left.
But curiously, she saw him putting off his goodbye,
she felt the ties that bind him to her.
The girl friend said: "we'll have tea at home Paul."
And she saw him looking at her unsure . . .
but knowing he must go.

Real Freedom

The attitude to the victim,
the one whose story of humiliation and pain brings forth such
feelings of care,
is so different to the response to the attacker,
the one whom society punishes harshly.
Polar opposites, or so they appear,
these crimes of brutality and cowering fear.
The onlooker judges without a second thought the one who vents his anger,
but uses much softer words to try to find a way to ease the pain of the other.
The hurter and the hurt who appear so separate,
are bound hand and feet.
Seeing themselves as separate,
it has them entrapped.
What is it that demands suffering,
and blindfolds them to keep them in the dark.
Love and nurturing of their own inner garden,
is what is missing.
One day these two will see,
that they too can be free.
How long will it be,
before they stop reacting and start acting.
What joy they'll find,
that first time they stop to look within to ease their pain.
For these two at last there will be release,
and love of self holds the key.
Then this partnership of love and hate,
this journey of madness will end.

Everybody should have an Uncle Frank

Everybody should have an Uncle Frank.
He ate pies with his hands while scanning the form.
Horses to an Irishman,
are more than just born.
The wireless drones on,
and this one doesn't pip the post.
For him politics and those Labor boys,
were always a topic of debate.
A look of concern furrowed his brow to give those Libs scorn.
But lately his fury was more for his own,
he couldn't relate to the Labor of today.
He'd rather remember those days when you'd fight for a mate.
With those Irish Delaney's you knew where you stood.
And Frank didn't stop fighting, right up till the end.
Bless the old bastard, he died with one leg.

Living on the Edge

Living on the edge of nowhere,
no calm, no soothing softness, no peace.
Longing for a soft touch, a kind word,
hanging in there, knowing it will pass.
The ache of her heart cuts deep, she feels chilled to the core.
Yet out the window, the sounds of spring are everywhere.
The birds are chirping, the flowers are in bud,
and the tips of new green give her a feeling of hope and joy.
She sees that her inner world could be compared to the changing
seasons in a garden,
constantly surprising and renewing.
But she's in a passage, a tunnel,
and the light of understanding is a little way off yet,
emotional trauma, midlife crisis, marriage breakdown, son leaving
home. It's all come together.
And the ties that bind are to her children.
She's wondering what is left behind.

Season's End

She did not want to go on this errand. Her body did not want to go there.
But she knew she must.
This house had come to an end of its life and she felt the pain of the
one who had lived there and could no more.
That was enough.
But the pain of grown grand-children whose memories of love and
caring etched deep was also deeply felt.
They did not want to let go. They wanted to stop time.
It was not allowed this cruel destruction of a cherished childhood.
And who was she . . . this stranger who came and pushed them to let go.
She did not know why she was there. Surely some support for her
husband who was winding up his childhood home.
He needed her she knew that.
But this one who came like an overseer of death was trembling inside.
It felt too hard to her too.
Only once did she stay overnight in that house that was decaying and
derelict.
Painting over a lifetime of memories.
When she finally left that morning her entire being was sighing with relief.
There was no more she could do. It was enough.
She knew in her heart the sadness of everyone and especially of the
man who would not come home to his sanctuary again.
Life can be cruel. It giveth and taketh away.
One day it would be her turn to let go. And there would be others to
clean up the material corpse for her.
Over and over this scene is played out everywhere and
with everyone. No one can avoid this fate.
Like the tree in the forest the soul enjoys the seasons, year after year.
Then one day the tree roots no longer receive sustenance from the
earth and its spirit soars free.
And what is left is firewood.

A Celebration of Black

Today my thoughts turned to that black pansy.
So striking amidst the sunnier shades that speak to the soul of
happiness within,
a natural flowering of diversity, where nothing is excluded.
No thought of interfering with this prolific selection.
So, in life, this one who seems so imperfect, so lost,
who plays the part no body wants.
Who is to say nay to this brave one,
not afraid to be black.
Humanity may turn to exclude . . .
and hide its face,
from such a confrontation.
And yet there are those among us who smile and include and welcome,
who know we all play an important part in this beautiful kaleidoscope.
Of that one perfection . . .
life itself.

To the Birthday Girl

Friendship is something you can't make up,
it is there or it is not.
You know when it is because the link withstands everything,
no matter how long the separation.

Thankfully it comes as a gift,
that is always fresh.

In my case my friend is also my cousin,
we go back a long way,
from gurgling babies to now rather over-ripe apples.

She's 60 now and so am I,
it is with a sense of gratitude that I realize today, at her birthday
celebration, that maybe we have known
each other the longest.

If I had to answer the question of what makes her so special I would
find it hard to pinpoint one thing,
she has many fine qualities.
But for me, it is her sense of humor and that infectious,
hilarious laugh.
Seriousness doesn't survive long around Trisha,
but who she is and how good her presence makes us feel does.

My Mum

Woke up quiet and sad,
missing the physical body of my mother so deeply.
Her arms, her face,
old and wrinkled,
but so lovely,
so very lovely,
Just to touch her again,
never to be.
My heart weeps and weeps, the pain of parting from her,
her her-ness, so unique, so cherished.
And how to make that switch,
from the body to the spirit.

True Seeing

There comes a time when an inner shift takes place,
it shifts the focus or perspective to the opposite polarity.
Where once what was wrong ate
into your being, and brought with it
the pain of anger and frustration.
There now comes riding in a different horse,
with a big powerful message to spread.
All of a sudden, it is what was so right that eats into your heart,
and you feel a different kind of pain.
A remorseful, sensation of gratitude,
for your mother and the world.
Not anymore a focus on what's missing,
but what was there all along.

God Bless and Goodnight

Some warmth crept back into my heart last night,
felt a shift in my heart centre,
like someone had come and taken out my heart and warmed it.
Such a change,
after weeks of reliving my mum's passing.
Witnessing the slow ebbing away of her physical body once was
cruel enough.
Seeing the life drawn slowly out from her,
someone I love so much,
had me so tight,
held in fright,
with no hope of flight.
My breathing is deepening at last,
God bless and goodnight.

The Realm of the Heart

Love and pain so entwined,
cannot be separated.
Who tries to do so,
will face cremation.
No one but a fool,
would try.
Only the very brave,
love with every fibre of their being.
They live in the realm of the heart.
ready to break,
and ready to mend.
Whenever life and the heart's longing,
makes the fire,
this one walks barefoot on the coals.
And laughs and weeps,
and is ready to love,
again and again . . .

Wake-Up Call

Late at night,
hadn't been well,
a restlessness inside me,
tossing and turning in the bed.
Spirit whispered from somewhere,
. . . forget feeling good and comfort,
find . . . "that" which is never born,
and "that" . . . which never dies.

Teacher in Disguise

The human response to a dog has me entertained.
He is just a dog.
Yet, so many different opinions to his nature.
Some visitors come in quietly and respectfully and comment how
gentle and loving is this brown curly dog.
He is a really beautiful dog, they say, as they leave.
Others seem friendly but the body language offends and this same
dog is barking and protective of his place and family.
It is as if this humble dog sees what comes in with the person.
This fastness, that is oblivious of life around them, has him hurrying to
the soft rug in the bedroom.
To the one that has observed him since a pup it is an education.
Angry people get an angry response.
Gentle people get a gentle response.
People full of fear get something to be afraid of.
Rough play may end up with a nip.
And there are those who get too close without his permission and the
warning bark sends them startling backwards.
Does he have multiple personalities,
or is he just reflecting what is in front of him.
So who is this brown curly dog who lovingly licks my hand and rests
his head on my leg.
Who knows how to be happy with the simple things.
A teacher if you take time to watch and listen.

Into Me See

Pictures flash by,
of a man bearing flowers.
Of happy times,
sometimes sunny, sometimes showers.

No attachment, just enjoying the moment,
wishing still for a love that binds,
but happy with her own flowering.

Walking on the beach,
enjoying the busy, city, café scene.
Talking of moods and changes,
always open to the leaving.

One day she saw his attention shift,
it was gone in a flash.
How did she feel!
This one who gave her love freely and let go.
Smiling, yet saddened,
she knew her picture show of past memories,
of love and pain and letting go,
was always there.

She just had to look,
and let go.

Blessed Be

All opinions, especially mine,
are odious.
What a different world it would be without opinions.
Opinions on their own are not bad,
but our attachment to them,
creates separation on a world-wide scale.
Blessed be those who opinions don't matter to them.

Nothing to Say

There are those who live out their lives with a deep secret,
while others shout about sexuality as being who they are.
Others who don't fit the norm say nothing at all.
Not one word is spoken.

Stress and Blaming

Whenever I am stressed,
for whatever reason.
There is no one to blame,
especially not me.

True Heroes

The love that has no form.
What seems like ugliness,
pain and struggle,
is the miracle of life itself.
Born to live, born to die,
entry and exit.
No concept of future,
no idea of what comes next.
Just diving down that birth canal,
and at the end of life,
exiting to that unknown place.
Where spirit needs no body,
just is.

Compassion

When you give up pretending you have it all together,
you start to feel much closer to the human race.
Other peoples' so-called shortcomings,
just become what they are working through,
you wish them well.
And you view your own personal mistakes,
in a much more gentle way.

No Rules in Love

They were in a world of their own.
Watching, it was hard to separate,
the dance from the dancer.
Perfectly in step, moving as one body,
up close and personal.
Many nights of practice,
two minds working as one,
plus an eagerness to go with the flow.
The ballroom dancers held the audience in their trap.
He was a gay man and she was straight,
nobody noticed that.
But his sister knew,
she had watched them over many years
and knew their love was true.
It broke all the rules,
and even in their parting,
when she found a lover who wanted a family,
still love was there.
Life moved on and he had many other male partners,
and one day he died.
He had very few possessions,
in his drawer were two photos.
One of the day he married her,
and another of them on the ballroom floor,
dancing together as one.

Bursting

Such a love in my heart,
even when words wound me and others,
this love does not diminish.
Burning, burning, burning,
so much happens in this presence,
polarities switching from moment to moment.
But so still and eternal is this love,
some longing to touch it,
to be close,
but it is not allowed.
It is taboo to bring the body into this.

Truth Revealed

Can it be lost,
this ocean of stillness.
Once revealed,
it is as solid as a healthy heart beat.
The surface can be anything at all,
a wild sea, a violent storm,
a lazy ocean lapping the shore.
The same can be said of this me,
this identity,
all the moods.
But on the inside,
no me. no moods.
let it be.
No where to go,
just to be aware of the lies,
the grasping, the hiding,
the reaching.
Be willing to directly experience the mirage,
to rediscover the omnipresent stillness,
the essence of all that is.

Heart-speak

My heart is speaking so loudly this evening.
Telling me what it needs to survive.
Not about what has to be done, or even survival.
But how precious, precious, time is,
when spent with the one who is loved so dearly.
Some would call it quality time,
a day a week,
when all other considerations are ignored.
A day we share the nurture of nature,
something so softening and pleasing to the spirit,
that the tears fall like rain.
You can feel it in your chest,
hearts have to commune,
they have to soften,
they have to weep.
They have to feel and
what is left is fullness,
fullness to the very core.
There is no depth to life without this.
Love is the antidote to all pain,
and the tears are full of joy.

Subtle Switch

Turning the mind back,
a subtle switch of perception,
revealed this spaciousness,
this peace.
This deep, deep love,
and relaxation.
One minute the mind gears up to create distractions,
then a simple movement,
turning the mind inward,
back to the creator,
and all illusion vanished.
Just spaciousness,
no me, no object,
just sublime peace, the nectar of the gods.

So Still

A day of quiet,
so still, unable to even witness.
Just breathing,
all agitation of the mind,
so far away.
So distant, like something,
somewhere in the haze.
No attempt to look,
can't move.

No engine to start up any doing,
so no-one to start a thought.
Too hard . . . let it be.
A death, a dying,
no trying.
Little by little I am disappearing,
and life as I knew it is over.
Just be still.
What peace, what a relief,
no more to do.

Body Meditation

Aware of a trumpet,
and I was looking through a small hole at one end,
as it widened out to the world.
That this witness is who I really am,
and that it never dies.
My throat was on fire on one side,
so dry and hot I coughed.
I thought I might have to go out and leave this meditation,
but went up into my awareness,
and watched the feeling as it settled.
Then this wind started to pop from my mouth,
and air was rising up from my stomach,
the fire moved to my left ear,
burning then subsiding.
More poppy breaths, then quiet.
Very present and aware,
that my body had let go of something.
And my spirit felt better for it.

Friend and Lover

Some soft remembering,
of making love.
The merging of him and I,
the soft love and finally of the passion spent.
But more eerie it was,
to watch him move,
like a walking dream,
across the bedroom.
I fell into a trance remembering,
of making love many, many times with this one.
How many times,
and how many lifetimes,
I wondered.

Back seat driver

Sometimes in long-term relationships,
your parents' pattern lives again.
Getting along with the other,
can be like going against your flow.
It can leave the supportive one feeling dry,
like she is driving from the back seat.
She feels the urge to take the wheel
and steer life in a softer direction.
Even as this thought arises,
she smiles and notices,
there is nothing to do.
She's already beginning
to tack her new direction,
in so many little ways.

So much gratitude

What an experience,
looked into that place of peace,
and every now and then,
my mind would stir.

Trying to go down that old road of thought,
and bang it would just run out of steam.
It was too hard,
so much easier to sit in,
that well of stillness.

Since then I am more awake,
than I have ever been.
And every now and then,
for no reason I am back in that well.
Basking in the power of sitting,
in that ocean of stillness.

I can't move,
even when my mind stirs,
to get me busy.
It just doesn't have any power.
I am this spaciousness,
and it is all-embracing.
No boundary between me and it,
no form, nothing to do.

So much gratitude,
how many masters must I thank.
Thank you all.
I bow down to the feet of the one,
that led me to this simple wonder.

I kiss your feet,
you are welcome to have my head.
This heart is then free to love and give thanks.
truly, free.
Happy I am,
free I am,
I am the infinite in all I see.
Oh, yes I am.
Hallelujah.

Wake-up call

What if there was nothing wrong.
That all the so-called imperfection—
in ourselves and others,
is just a mirage.
A disguise,
that seduces us,
from time to time.
Into a belief that is not real,
not true.
How we would smile,
and laugh,
at how much time has been spent,
lost to ourselves,
chasing invisible shadows.
We would wake-up,
like finger-snap.
And a life in the shadows,
would be no more.

Michael rowed the boat ashore . . .

I know what it is like to lose a brother,
you keep on remembering,
the chubby-faced smiling baby,
that as it grew older never lost its' sweet smile.
It was a 'happy to be in the background kind of smile',
that took great joy in another's good fortune.
There was this generousity of spirit,
that just loved to share the good times.
He was most happy on the water in his boat,
anyone who had the good fortune to be on board,
was sure to have a day to remember,
there would be fish and adventure a plenty.
He loved to share and he loved to help,
and yet he had some pain he could not share.
Over the years too much partying,
with a Bundy in his hand,
stripped away his health and his sanity.
Even so he could pull himself up,
to please those who loved him.
His loving spirit never gave up on giving,
arriving back with a good catch,
it would soon be gone—
shared with neighbors and friends.
This rebel had no fear,
and in his younger days he broke the rules.
He only knew one speed,
and that was flat out.
When the police car gave chase to try and catch him,
he gave them a run for their money.

'Don't worry', his love said to me:
'he'll be home later, they will never catch him'.
They never did,
but somehow life did.
Right up to the end his presence shone.
He was and is our Michael,
Our darling brother.
We miss him so.

Dream

Dreamt about the light of Jesus,
shining from his heart,
out through his body,
to the whole world.

Who Gives

To give,
and to give,
from a pure place.
No doer,
no me.
What a party,
that would be.

*May all beings
everywhere
be happy*